Lovesick

Lily Bowman

BookLeaf Publishing

India | USA | UK

Presentation by *BookLeaf Publishing*

Web: www.bookleafpub.com

E-mail: info@bookleafpub.com

ISBN: 9789357691819

First edition 2022

DEDICATION

For those I've never stopped loving.

ACKNOWLEDGEMENT

Thank you to my friends that serve as endless encouragement, and my parents for bearing with me through it all.

PREFACE

Who knew one heart could hold so many words.

Empty

Blanket blank space
all erase any casket you'd previously held in
mind.

A chronicle of emptiness with which to breathe
deep
and then with sudden hitching
expel
the very thing momentarily ago you thought you
couldn't do without.

Crumbs

I fall in love too easily
with your ideosyncracies
your sighing eyes over coffee steam

As I sit
a stranger to you.

In love as soon as you share a piece, a crumb, of
your soul with me.
Just one morsel and forever I love
far past the lingering gaze through shuttlebus
haze
long after I should not forgive any further

forget not in my heart's vocabulary
as much as my memory wavers

I stay in love far too long.
when it's bitter as day old coffee
sitting amidst towers of unwashed dishes
still my heart belongs scattered along the city
so it can never truly be mine
or yours
unless you're asking?

Shitkickers

Throbbing beating bombasting ballistic beneath
boots
Hard rubber soled, peeling, cracked like bark on
an old maple
and reliable.

I stomp out a tattoo marching down pavement in
my all seasons
nothing can stop us once we're rolling

Sunshine music and a hand to hold
are all that set shitkickers skipping

Inevitable

Love lies weeping where love once lay in liar's
arms
This soul seeping
over the bed spilling
onto the tile
in puddles of moaning ecstasy a moment away
from sheer grief

It is impossible to love
without the inevitability of heart break looming
overhead

That we still dance
as thunder roars all around
is the immutable beauty of humanity.

Romancing Writer's Block

Inspiration walks along the tender fine line
replacing foot after printed trail
spider-like along silk strands
forever chasing the muse.

And all I've ever seen is a slight smile over a
whisper of a shoulder.

Catching Feelings

Forever unsettled
bubbling sewage seeping through the cracked
foundation I stand on.
No home with which to call upon.

Rage wells up from the basement
like a cracked pipe
and pollutes my mind.

Fear follows close,
it's stench creeping like fog up the stairs.

Profound Sadness descends
so similar to a soft snowfall on the roofs of
semi-detached two-family homes.

And Apathy finds her way through the front
door with the key I gave her.

Aching

How do you breathe
when it's all smoke?

How do you scream
when your throat chokes?

How can I live
when the edge is so close?

How,
when now it's all broke.

The Fall

It's nice to meet you
Autumn death so sweet and sad
Your touch will haunt on.

Joy

My face hurts

from not anything it hasn't felt before

Yet these bursts of Joy,
what makes falling in love so tempting,
kill my cheeks

in a way that I used to feel in my eyes
sunken into myself
So man days of fear thinning my jaw

Receding inward.

As much weight and essence lost,
I'd like to bombastically laugh and grin my heart
out loud.

Happiness rarely makes for good poetry.

Skyway

Night lights
of city bright
and sparkling

Howling traffic
dropping pressure suddenly

The sky, a deadened pool of dark
against misty long evening withdrawing toward
midnight

Sound pops back in

Cityscapes glittering over the water
recalling sunlit caps
hinting at hallmark memories.

The crush of humanity piling in
once the bridge is past
lonely roads curved down
and the light is on in the window

Monday

Feed your insecurities
wash down the hierarchy of needs

In

Out

Wind pushed past

and long

through these cracked lips
that so many have descecrated

Just a jolt

Like a memory brought on by smell

Quell these instincts that fly me off the wall
and back again
scratching down my face

Never was any good at love songs

Meltdown

Noise

Clanking in

as the plastic clock arms go by
a hum of song from the kitchen
tinkles of T.V.
and huffing communications from the dog

hardwood floors hold my focus

trying to ground

and stop remembering exactly how hard a floor
like this can feel
bruises on bruises on the back of my head
so I can never forget

overwhelmed is an understatement

I cannot scream here

Sleepless Night

Ephemeral

like dust motes

that clichés float between time passing

as such

five past midnight

and never another thought

(beyond that on the highway)

of wishes

as time trickled

and thrashed

in near nine traffic.

Is the day over yet?

Perception

Silence of sweeping winds
outside the sudden daylit windowpane

Like the rushing of blood in my ears when life is
inescapable.

Leaves pouring off the treetops in some
incomprehensible dance that poets ascribe
meaning to.

Generally unsuccessfully.

How do you romance autumn into significance?

Simple observation circumnavigating the heart.

Should On You

it shouldn't hurt so much
to rip off Band-Aids
when that's what healing looks like

it shouldn't hurt so much
to rebreak a bone
when it's set the wrong way
and causes pain every day

it shouldn't hurt
when I walk away
and you call me names

but that's not the way of the world now is it?

Entropy

I peel myself apart
looking for where I went wrong
what part of me is stinking
where is the sinew that snapped
and drove you off the edge

Love me through yesterday

You were right when you told me not to listen to
his messages

to delete them

You were right telling me he's just throwing a
tantrum

it's nothing to do with me

You were right to make sure he brought my
things to our one last goodbye

which he didn't

You were right when you said he'd be waiting
for me

nothing happened

You were right
And I didn't listen

Help

I've fallen in love again
help me up
I can't stay down here

Not when your eyes
are forest pools
reflecting the sunken treasure

Not when your lips speak the softest sweets

Not when your shoulders
hold a lifetime
and still stoop to save my toes the stretch

Not when you're my tree to shelter
because what do I do when the thunder comes
and I have nowhere to run?

Help

My foolish heart is too eager
like a fresh fighter in the ring
a masochist of the worst variety
no scarring
outside the criss-crossing on my organs

So please

Help

I've fallen in love again
tripped stumbled careened and crashed
and this time
How do I even get up?

Lest I forget how it feels
to have the floor leave me
when you plant kisses on my brow

or how your arms wrap me a delicate cage
with the doors wide open

How do I bandage bruises from the fall
when you taste is still fresh
and I'm tonguing the empty spot I've made.

With Teeth

That smile
cracking over the horizon of your face
it's sunny rays
warm the frost of late midnight dew

Leaving

You're not allowed to do this

I'm the one who breaks hearts

And there you are standing still

As I leave

And somehow this is all your fault

A Lone Lover

So here I sit

Alone

Desperate to not be lonely

What my mum
and my friends
and my therapist
all warned me of

To not occupy my bed for the sake of warming
my winters

Maybe this time around I'll learn to love myself
alone.

www.ingramcontent.com/pod-product-compliance
Lightning Source LLC
LaVergne TN
LVHW021350200726
843509LV00014B/2772